Somewhere Dawn is Rising

Poetry

Courtney L. Smith

Paperback: ISBN 978-1-0881-6426-6

First paperback edition August 2023

Cover Design, Layout and Editing by
Courtney L. Smith

For the dreamers and gentle hearts looking for a soft place to land.

Contents

Author's Note

Dear Reader,

This text contains darker themes*, magical realism, and a
hefty dose of imagination.
While the majority of poems explore the beauty of nature,
life, and love- contrast reveals itself to offer depth in the
scope of human emotion and what it means to be alive.

There are two ways to read this book-
page by page or you can travel through the seasons from
spring to winter on the left side with haiku and then read the
poems on the right side.

Any likeness to real people is purely coincidental unless you,
like me, consider the actors of one's imagination to be
friends.

x

*death, grief

Rising

The last of winter fades
my soul awakens
dormant in the undergrowth
reaching, I break ground
as old man winter
ambles away

The keeper of sleep
and bones chilled knee-deep
he drags the chains behind him
catching on vines
through the garden of time
I watch until he's gone

And then I rise
with fresh spring eyes
to stretch toward the dawn

wildflowers rise
rebirth and renewal
nests of speckled eggs

Sunset

The sun set into a pool
of honeyed nectarine
while the sky
dripping in pastels
deepened into sapphire
sparkling with light
of infinite stars

Each glint seducing revelers
speckled on the sandy shore
and the moon
the new moon-
a hair so thin and so bright
it looked as though I
punctured the night sky
with my thumb nail
to let the light in
from another realm

lingering daylight
spring rains nourish soil and seed
earth births promises

Riding in on Nighttide

We came riding in
on nighttide
black sky
black water
stars reflected
back and forth
a volley of fire
faded years ago
it dazzled
it caught us in
the aether
between two worlds
the space grew
beneath her
swimming
this way
that
lost to the tide
of a rising dawn
we ride

between earth and blossom
an essence of love hums
a divine lullaby

Watercolor

The room swam with watercolor
a medley of tones
in the veneer of light
streaming in from the garden
thick pale beams flooded
trails of floating dust
breathing became palpable
as we watched our breath
guide the air
life felt like a Renoir painting
brush strokes highlight
cheekbones and vases
of billowing bouquets
we were art
the universe sheathed
in tender flesh
to know where we ended
and the world began
was indistinguishable

spring tucked winter in
earth's abundance rises up
to greet a new dawn

Still Going

The weight piles on
soft dirt packs into mud
as I outstretch my hands
to feel the heat of the sun

The cold, dark earth rests
atop my shallow lungs
Even here I'm not alone
The miserly world has won

I thought I have abandoned
all that drains my soul
worms gather 'round
digging hole by hole

Something pulls me from the soil
As I squint into the light
Every word I haven't written
Lifts me to sit upright

There are things left unfinished
I must see to the end
So today is not the day
I retreat into the land

a soft mist rinses
leaves and bark to reveal a
world rich in color

We Will Love Well

When the world ends
we will love well

it is only then
when all's been felled

broken and burned
earth an empty shell

will the dawn rise
and love will swell

into the space
it could not fill

when all was lost
to hostile thrills

hold fast
don't let your breath still

for when the world ends
we will love well

early may rain
tapping at the window panes
spring bulbs flowering

Flower Path

Down the flower path
I'm roaming
daylight fades to
silent gloaming
the pace I step
begins on slowing
I stop to look around

The world has shifted
it's overflowing
a humming wind swells
now it's blowing
I touch a petal
it's started glowing
there's magic in the ground

little green neck bent
rising toward the spring sun
the hills come alive

Incantation

Around we dance
under the waxing moon light
burnished fair visions
carried through night
white dress, white hair
the sabbat was near
the bonfire grew
and we laced our hands
with a ribbon blue
I heard the voices
from inside the flames
an incantation of love
to which we add our names

wild coastal wind
seagrass waves to the sea
gulls beckon the sun

Before We Go

We know
this will all end
and we will
find ourselves
at the end of
the walk
turning to wave
to no-one
to everyone
for our time here
is spent
and into the light
we fly
so before
we make it
down that way
look around
give love
accept love
breathe love
it is the only
way home

california
covered in orange poppies
mirror of the sun

Ars Longa Vita Brevis

Our lives-
a single breath
exhaled by the world
we capture it
and with our hands
shape it into something tangible
beautiful evidence
of our transience
a fragment of our perception
and like the stars
our creations trail behind
etched in the
landscape of time

you will live forever
a story never finished
by the stroke of my pen

Immortal

The marble halls echoed
of our whispers growing
in silence of stone-etched gods
there laid a knowing
carved to perfection
the wind kept blowing
round and round the room

Ivy stretched and
kept on flowing
the viridian glass
of the wide open ceiling
shone a light
in which you're glowing
and I grabbed your hand to dance

We spun around the busts
never slowing
I heard your words
softly intoning
your truest longing
a gracious invoking
poetry into the air

sprouting wildflowers
gentle perfume swirling 'round
warm afternoon sun

Night Garden

In the pale light
of my night garden

petals white
blooms wide
glimmer under
the crystal sky

inhale the dew
of moonflower
take two
and let it flow through
your touch

to see your fate
slow your heart rate
and it will show
your truth

offering honey
the wheel turns to summer
flames dance under stars

Goddess Bath

I submerge into the brew
of a late summer dew
combined with herbs and flora

Chamomile and vines
mingle with needles of pines
to finely tune my aura

With the wisdom of plants
this pool of water grants
a power old as time

An honor of the world
bestowed through water swirled
from goddesses divine

mastering brilliance
your bodies paint the landscape
a spring eruption

But a Flame

We are all just flames
dancing and flickering
until a single gust
extinguishes us

Sweet firelight
burn bright
tonight is not
the night

sip of chamomile
birdsong carries us away
the day stretches long

Wisdom

Wisdom is to know
there are many lives
you could have lived
and the path you chose
may not be the one you'd choose today
but the one that was right at the time

So sure-footed as you ventured down the trail
to now pause for water and take in the view
only to see a distant vein in the landscape
more enticing, more fitting for the you
that you are now

And you can stand there and gaze at it
longingly, feeling your heart cracking
just a little
or you can keep forging ahead
with the wisdom in knowing that
they could easily merge
beyond the river

swaying under trees
the view is cobalt blue
leaves rustle above

A Self Portrait

I am nature
I am the earth
the trees and flowers
I'm the wind and the breeze
flowing with rivers and seas
I'm the elements in atoms
binding together in human form
I am the light of the sun
the reflection of the moon
and the buzz in faint bee wings
I am the pattern on butterfly wings
Dew drops on grass blades
I am nature healing nature
One breath at a time

laundry on the line
gardens abundant with choice
picnics in the shade

Grief
To those I love who feel loss

I wish I could hold your
tender life-stained heart
in the palm of my hand
and stroke it back to life-
to let the softness of my touch
shape it back to its youthful wholeness
assuring you that beauty still lives
and the place your love resides within
the heavy chambers of your body
is enough to keep them alive

the echoes of your gaping wounds
call to the heavens
waving like a mirror toward the sun
an SOS to alert your kindred souls
and how lovely to know that they see you
and your name is embedded in heaven
by the spirit you were so strong to let go
so not only are they still with you
but you are still with them when
they carried a piece of you
to paradise

the hours stretch long
as long as our shadows
backlight by starlight

Summer

We were idle
sprawled on coarse sand
and pebbles
seaside
one summer afternoon
books in hand
shading our eyes from
the blazing sun

Crashing waves- our melody
gulls the chorus
to lie here and listen
turning pages
of the world
behind our eyes
time ceased
hollowed

under the warm sea
the mottled surface glistens
sun rays filter through

3 a.m.

Are any thoughts
more holy than those
from the pillow at 3 a.m.

truth flows by the light of the moon
the desires of one's heart
more easily than in the light of day

it's here your dreams speak
guiding you toward
the stars that spark them

as an offering
for bearing the weight
of mortality

cicadas buzzing
summer afternoon chorale
pebbled ice in cups

Tethered

I am tethered
to heaven
slung here
down to earth
to live by the name
of some other god

vine at my back
frayed and weathered
one pull
we're severed
wings torn - hidden
tucked into my spine
the truth forbidden

gospel rides in
on wind and rain
to destroy beliefs
pearls of arcane
veins flowing with
mercury
here to reign

I held promises
like dandelion clocks
ready to take wind

A Promise

The tail of summer idles
softly swaying beyond our grasp
letting us linger a while longer
savoring warmth of the setting sun
as the water temperature dips
skin tingles with thrills of rushing waves
growing intensely toward winter's tide
I release a promise to the wind
to always see the world so beautiful
vibrant as the glowing sun
peaceful as settled sands
the words swirl around my head
tickling my lashes as they pass
off into the sunset
I feel I can breathe
at last

we were wild and free
by light of summer's hour
living poetry

Salon of Yore

There's a portal to another realm,
skeleton key lodged in the door.
When opened, a buttery backlit chatter,
of conversations long ago.
I hear the records spinning, scratching as they slow.
Haunting echos of the gramophone,
an air thick with tobacco.

As silhouettes grow along the wall, hours pass us by.
Glasses clink and laughter sparks,
dancing through the night.
I wait for the perfect moment,
to enter through the door.
To feel the enchanting ambience,
when the twenties roared.

I slip through the crack,
getting lodged somewhere between.
Hopeful, I reach out for help, but largely go unseen.
I'm struck- perhaps it's me,
the ghost cornered down the hall.
The energy of light, that doesn't exist at all. The room quiets
down, into the early morning air.
I return to our side,
with lingering smoke-scented hair.
Not an hour has passed, since I left this world,
to experience a charming era, one which I want to hold.

garden by moonlight
blanket of stars unfold
the sky devours me

Feast

Is it feast or famine
when you sit down at the table
outstretching your arms
to see if you are able-
to collect all it is you want
and everything you desire
is the food only for thought
or just to admire-
one day we wake up
and know this is it
eat the grape
don't let it slip-
our dreams cannot wait
the only time is now
take the leap of faith
it does not matter how-
what matters is you did it
you took the step ahead
weaving the fabric of your life
earnestly thread by thread

days soaked in sun rays
saltwater lures the fevered
ease sets in at last

Honey

My wistful hands skim tenderly
over jagged thorns to hold
a petite source of beauty
in this dispiriting world

Petals varnished in evening light
with an aromatic allure
each breath pulls me closer
curling in for more

Golden sun rays and honeyed buds
distill life into my palm
absolute in its simplicity
rests my heart beat calm

When endurance fades for this season in time
I know I can retreat a spell
inside this velvet light of mine
where all is warm and well

there is only one
chance to set the world alight
step into the fire

The Open Sea

Take me out
to the open sea
I'll let my arms
lay wide and free
atop the swells
I float alone
in the deep
I will atone

My hair drifts round
filtering light rays
like the seaweed below
each strand sways
diving down
the fish swim by
as I look toward
the blurry sky

Let me stay
under the sea
where silence
is a song to sing
sirens distant
watch over me
as I glide along
at last set free

hope lies between clouds
baring the face of the sun
warm rays filter through

Happiness

My happiness
is fleeting
it comes like
shifting dappled light
on a warm summer lawn
I move my blanket around
to catch it
to feel it faintly
kiss my skin
between the gusts of
a shady august wind

dawn of the harvest
bless the bounty before us
spirit of the grain

To Rise Again

I thought it was over
on that cold tile floor
looking toward the ceiling
hoping-
to penetrate it with my gaze
to find something, anything
divine reaching out to cradle me
and tell me

It will all be okay

The roof remained solid
unable to fulfill my wish
but I was drained of all sorrow
all life
with a steady stream of tears
releasing all my fears
so I could rise again
in the morning

I have always lived
in the tide of your emotions
waves that ruled the seas

Luminesce

I like to imagine
that night under the stars
we were brighter than
anything in the cosmos

together we shined
and somewhere up there
we were the beacon in
the atmosphere

years have turned to weeds
wading through the wilderness
sunrise offers hope

What is Time

Sometimes when spring
carries a chill through the air
I pretend it's an autumn evening

when the summer heat has gone
the leaves start falling
and the air begins weaving

scents of magic and spice
chimneys trickle with smoke
and the skeptics start believing

when the veil starts thinning
and the mystics begin crafting
new ways of perceiving

the reality of time
which is that it is everything
yet nothing at all

trees ripe for harvest
apple pie and cinnamon
air of mystery

Heat Wave

It was late summer and the air thick-
a stifling hug sticking to our skin

as the sun set the crickets mellow-
their days work of bodily hymns
alongside the whir of strained fans
was all that was left

it felt like time swelled into a
sultry golden orb ready to burst-
freeing us into the forgiving night
with a gentle hum lulling us to sleep

leaf covered sidewalks
candle light outgrows the sun
rainy windowpane

Cuyamaca

The dusty hillside glowed in that
California gold rush sort of way
with rusty brown and sienna hued curves
after a time without rain

warm afternoon winds drew warmer breaths
as I spread out on the boulder
listening to buzzing insects in nearby brush-
my hair draped over granite
untamed, coalescing with the backdrop

there was a trickling remainder
of early spring's stream
just enough to cool toes after
a long hike through labyrinthine trails

I remember thinking I found it-
life out here in the wild
the gold they were all after
that you can't carry home

souls of yesteryear
dwell beyond the iron fence
burnished leaves drift by

Deep Rest

It was the kind of summer morning
steeped in gilded light
that I could laze in the tall sweet grass
stirring with life
listening to birds and crickets
harmonizing their wild song

The air within inches of the earth
feels thick- like a warm exhale
from her fiery lungs deep below
a soothing contrast to the cool
soft soil in which I dig my toes
and I melt into that liminal space
between earth and sky

cinnamon sticks dipped
in freshly pressed cider
crisp air and sweaters

Rebirth

That night I vanished
all that I was
all that I knew
dissolved with my heart-
the last grains of sand
slipping through the hourglass-
roaming in the silver light
under the same moon
and I became nothing
or I became everything-
rearranged into
someone or something
new

twilight took over
black cats slip into shadows
ghostly winds blow wild

August

Heat holds while nudged
by cooler winds
leaves dry overhead on trees
not quite ready to let go
there's a richness in August
with it's golden eves
long shadows
and late summer dreams
the sun still strong
yet weakening
harvest season
unfolding

oak leaves turning gold
dodging falling acorns
squirrels laugh above

Summer Child

The large green electrical box
whirring where the sidewalks meet
in the flatlands of America
felt as good of a place as any to
sprawl out and watch the
clouds of summer speed by-
as the metal buzzed at my back
cumulus animals would roam
towing in a trifle storm
lasting only minutes to slice open
the humid air so we could breathe

Communal lawn freshly striped
north to south- leaving a chartreuse hue
around the soles of our shoes-
sidewalk barbecues sizzling
neighbors toss frisbees
dealing cards
sometimes I'd go to the tree not far away-
hang my small body from the lowest limb
and offer the spectacle of flight
whispering to the kids that
I can fly-
it was always the day the wind
wasn't just right to catch my fluttering arms
but "believe it to be true", I'd say.

ghouls, ghosts, and goblins
the veil between our worlds thin
vibrant hunter moon

Autumn

Copper and auburn leaves
a fine patina to the year
aged to perfection
a sweet confection
served to our eyes and ears

I wanted to know
on the other side of time
does it feel the same?

Unwritten

How many people
live parallel lives
out of fear
lives that could so easily
so beautifully
merge
into each other
if they were brave enough

How many love stories
were never written
because they lived behind
walls of apprehension
buried
by expectation
bars encasing their own
hearts
cages that could crumble
with the faintest
touch

leather bound books
steaming cups of coffee
dark skies brewing

Plight

I heard the owl's
wary call
twisted neck
in trees so tall
through the forest edge I run
into the midst
of the wild one
it shared a tale
a forewarning
of what the world
will be by morning
I went to town
to share the news
but they were rapt
with who is who
empty lives
on grand estates
trying to hide
from their fate

open the tea chest
spices and magic disperse
no longer captive

Ghost stories

In the heart of autumn
we'd spend our eves
out in the forest
amongst jeweled leaves

padding the floor
a seasonal bed
to spread out a blanket
and clear our heads

we'd light a fire
tell stories of ghosts
watching the winds
while marshmallows toast

did you hear that-
a howl beyond the trees
eyes of saucers scatter
before our voices cease

legend has it
our hearts raced us home
echoing through the forest
where all villains roam

add another log
chimney smoke mingles with snow
let the forest sleep

Distraction

In the shallows
the light shimmers
on the sand
of the shore-
do not shelter
for the shine
fades slowly
forevermore

silver moon above
illuminates the crystals
my breath escapes me

Seams

The seams of my soul
stretch taut
swelling
with dreams
passions and promises
that I continually
tuck deep inside
my body
and someday
I will burst

rest your darkness
wild crier of the night
land upon my hand

Swan Song

Autumn air feels
wondrously golden
I can almost hear
the clatter of particles
as they cooly whirl around
creating an opus with
the withering leaves
the swan song
of the year
crowning in hues of
pecan and cinnamon
traced with copper
listen to the incantations
of nature as it dissolves
into itself
letting go of haste
to one day soon
rise anew

pearls drip from eves
in a monotone world
pine perfumery

Winter

Have you ever looked up
when it's snowing
to see each flake falling
toward your face
eyes fill with ice
and the whole world blurs
alabaster
enveloped by winter
and you're the only one
on earth

biting winter air
cozy cabin under snow
the fire warms us

First of December

This is where the ice grows
stretching its dormant wings
spreading across wild bodies
of water and frigid things

Flakes of crystals drifting
down from the gray skies
winds twirl them 'round
before the pink sunrise

A world awakens to see white
a vision of winter's hold
it's icy fingers grasp the land
there's no shelter from the cold

winter sunlight weeps
a golden ink spread
honey in my palm

Rubies

Rubies slip from
her skin
to flush away
those who bore
deep within
her body

still swaying
in winter's wind
she stretches toward
the sun
her grand finale

they feed
on her softened flesh
rich marrow
of life
transfers from one
to another

hollowed
her sacred bones
stand
a skeleton
dripping rubies

children delighted
riding down the snow bank
a cardinal sings

Fallen Wood of Winter

Granted- it was a dead tree
bare limbed and old
standing in the wayside
forgotten by tending hands
but not by time-
woodpeckers fed on her inner core
of insects roaming
hole dotted spine-
doves, hummingbirds
swallows and finches took
rest on her limbs-
she framed the moon
in the dark skies
holding the lustrous ball-
a skeleton still thriving
with life- even if not her own
the sky now bare where
she once stood
birds keep passing through
no longer a haven or a home
to all who she once
reverently knew

enough umbrella
for one and a half persons
I'm always the half

Love

We are nature
composed
in sentience
to love the way
things should be loved
in this wild world
of magical things

frankincense and myrrh
feast beside the glowing log
holly king is crowned

Lantern

Night grew
the sky faded
cerulean to a deep violet
then indigo
and the stars popped
one by one
like holes
dotting a paper lantern

easier to see
the horizon through bare trees
leaves a memory

Home

When I tire of life
in this contrived world
I walk outside and lie down
under the soft gauzy sky
deep brown soil envelops me
blades of verdant grass
reach out for greeting
"welcome home" they say
as I close my eyes and rest
in nature's embrace

the earth lost color
a light snow flutters down
life fades to a dream

Wasteland

desolate wasteland
where tumbleweeds blow
sand stirs 'round
at my feet below

the air is thick
pale yellow
and it's hard to see
my way through

but in the distance
a dazzling light shines
landing on my face
to offer me the signs

do I walk toward it
or am I walking away
from the barren past
into eternity

winter solitude
warm drinks, books, and blankets
cabin in the woods

Introvert

I tolerate reality
while I toe the line
of humanity
and the realm in which
I naturally dwell

white-capped mountain range
frames a cold December sky
glossy morning sun

Seek

I woke by the light of the moon-
a sliver of a silver river flowing over me.
And I thought- is this all there is?
My mind raced through my life and the lives of others in
these night hours and I realized- yes, this really is all there is.

That is why we seek meaning and romance in the details. If
we don't fall in love with sunsets and ocean waves- if we
don't swoon at the sight of the moon- if we don't bathe
ourselves in the richness of earth's offerings-
Then yes, this is all there is.

festive records play
heard through storefront windows
air of nostalgia

Morning Hours

The morning hours
were my tonic
I'd drink them insatiably
when thick consternation
would dwell overhead
like dark, heavy clouds-
I'd light the oil lamp
at first blush of dawn
to watch the flame dance
with shadows upon the wall-
my shadow
looked freer than any
other hour
soaked in the freshness
of life, of chance of waking
it was the time when I
could be myself
no veil, no guise
no pretense-
it was my fading
shadow and I pirouetting
by candlelight
a subtle waltz to
breathe myself
back to life

soaring cedars
cloaked in freshly fallen snow
a sight to behold

Portal

After the heavy rain fell
one particular puddle
held the light with
a silvery reflection

Somewhere in its depths
I heard you calling
touching the surface
rippling
I reach
either to pull you through
or fall into

I did not know which
but I took the leap
for a chance to keep
this dream I keep
on dreaming

melting snow drips
streams begin to liven
grizzlies rise again

Moving On

Memories rattle around
in my bones
like rainsticks
that I try to shake
and loosen their hold

surging daffodils
streams awash with winter snow
birds sing with vigor

The Twenties

Keep your eyes
set far away
horizons wide
will not betray

one day at a time
they'd say
as darker clouds
would drift our way

we never stopped hoping
for the sun to shine
For the flowers to rise
or stars to align

it finally came
tasting bittersweet
nothing was the same
after such defeat

but we pressed on
in a world distressed
for a soft warm spot
to lie and rest

seeds stir underground
to greet the warming sun
earth thaws for new life

Air and Earth

When winter's pale skin
meets spring's fair buds
horizons tenderly blur
with ephemeral ease
as though this moment
had been long
anticipated by both

uniting of seasons
with one slight caress
of air and earth
to pass the baton
of beauty
and life

If you've enjoyed Somewhere Dawn is Rising, please consider writing a review on Amazon, Goodreads, or a platform of your choice. Your support is wildly appreciated.

Other books by the author -

Forest of Light - Poetry and Images on Nature and Life

Courtney L. Smith is a poet, photographer, calligrapher, yogi, mother, and nature lover living in Southern California. She spends her time musing on the seasons, surrounded by books, capturing life through her camera lens, building worlds in her mind, and spending time with her family.

You can find her at clsmithwriter.com or on her instagram at notestothewild.